STRATEGIC STUDIES INSTITUTE

The Strategic Studies Institute (SSI) is part of the U.S. Army War College and is the strategic-level study agent for issues related to national security and military strategy with emphasis on geostrategic analysis.

The mission of SSI is to use independent analysis to conduct strategic studies that develop policy recommendations on:

- Strategy, planning, and policy for joint and combined employment of military forces;

- Regional strategic appraisals;

- The nature of land warfare;

- Matters affecting the Army's future;

- The concepts, philosophy, and theory of strategy; and,

- Other issues of importance to the leadership of the Army.

Studies produced by civilian and military analysts concern topics having strategic implications for the Army, the Department of Defense, and the larger national security community.

In addition to its studies, SSI publishes special reports on topics of special or immediate interest. These include edited proceedings of conferences and topically oriented roundtables, expanded trip reports, and quick-reaction responses to senior Army leaders.

The Institute provides a valuable analytical capability within the Army to address strategic and other issues in support of Army participation in national security policy formulation.

i

Strategic Studies Institute
and
U.S. Army War College Press

UNITED STATES-GULF COOPERATION
COUNCIL SECURITY COOPERATION
IN A MULTIPOLAR WORLD

Mohammed El-Katiri

October 2014

*****

*****

Comments pertaining to this report are invited and should be forwarded to: Director, Strategic Studies Institute and U.S. Army War College Press, U.S. Army War College, 47 Ashburn Drive, Carlisle, PA 17013-5010.

*****

This manuscript was funded by the U.S. Army War College External Research Associates Program. Information on this program is available on our website, *www.StrategicStudies Institute.army.mil*, at the Opportunities tab.

*****

*****

The Strategic Studies Institute and U.S. Army War College Press publishes a monthly email newsletter to update the national security community on the research of our analysts, recent and forthcoming publications, and upcoming conferences sponsored by the Institute. Each newsletter also provides a strategic commentary by one of our research analysts. If you are interested in receiving this newsletter, please subscribe on the SSI website at *www.StrategicStudiesInstitute.army.mil/newsletter*.

FOREWORD

The ongoing impasse over development of nuclear and missile technologies by Iran highlights the continuing importance of U.S. security cooperation with Arabian Gulf states. Yet the rising economic strength and diplomatic assertiveness of some member states of the Gulf Cooperation Council (GCC) combines with potential political fragility there to require sensitivity by the United States in ensuring that cooperation continues to thrive.

In this monograph, British academic Dr. Mohammed El-Katiri analyzes the security and economic dynamics of the region as a whole, in order to assess the challenges to the security and military relationship between the GCC and the United States. He addresses the changing perceptions of U.S. military support among the local populations, and identifies a number of key areas where U.S. policy can adjust and add flexibility in order to pre-empt potential dilemmas.

This monograph was completed in September 2013, and therefore does not include mention of more recent developments such as the rise of the Islamic State or the November 2013 nuclear agreement with Iran. But the problems and themes it describes are permanent ones, and continue to present important considerations for protecting the interests of the United States and its allies in the region in the longer term.

The Strategic Studies Institute recommends this monograph to both the military and diplomatic policy communities as essential material to underpin sound policy decisions for the future of U.S. security relationships with the region.

DOUGLAS C. LOVELACE, JR.
Director
Strategic Studies Institute and
    U.S. Army War College Press

ABOUT THE AUTHOR

MOHAMMED EL-KATIRI is a Director of MENA Insight, a political risk consultancy that focuses on the Middle East and North Africa, and a Senior Research Analyst at the United Kingdom's (UK) Conflict Studies Research Centre (CSRC). Before joining CSRC, Dr. El-Katiri was a Research Fellow at the UK Defence Academy, and later served as a Political Risk Analyst at Eurasia Group and as a senior researcher at the Hague Institute for Global Justice. With more than 10 years of regional experience, his research interests include political and economic security in North Africa and the Gulf Cooperation Council (GCC) states, as well as North African relations with the European Union, and security policies around the Mediterranean. Dr. El-Katiri has published numerous internal and external UK Defence Academy reports, including reference papers on national and regional security issues in the GCC and the Mediterranean, and a monograph on the Algerian national oil and gas company Sonatrach. In addition, his publications include commentaries and research papers in a range of languages for research organizations in the UK and Europe, as well as various newspaper articles in and about the region. Dr. El-Katiri is a frequent commentator in media including the British Broadcasting Company, the *Financial Times*, and *Al-Jazeera*.

SUMMARY

Profound changes in regional geopolitical dynamics in the Arabian Gulf since the early-2000s render the region a highly challenging environment for U.S. foreign policy and military engagement. At a time of continuing domestic instability in Iraq and an increasingly isolated Iran, the geopolitical weight of the Gulf Cooperation Council (GCC) states has risen dramatically over the past 10 years; the GCC states' enormous economic power, coupled to some of the most stable political systems in the entire Middle East and North Africa region, call for continuously close U.S.-GCC relations in the security sphere as an important element in U.S. foreign policy.

But these fundamental shifts in the political environment coincide with changes in the regional perception of the United States as a security partner. The conflict in Iraq, resulting in yet another unstable state at the heart of the Middle East and in immediate proximity to the GCC, has left many former supporters of U.S. engagement in the region disappointed and cynical. Furthermore, ongoing U.S. defense budget adjustments have raised concerns among GCC leaders about the future of U.S. military capabilities and U.S. willingness and ability to engage in the region. In addition, U.S. responses to the Arab Spring sent important signals to the GCC about the potential durability of U.S. political and military support in the event of popular demand for more democratic rights and access to their countries' economic resources.

This monograph analyzes the security and economic dynamics of the region as a whole to assess the challenges to the security and military relationship between the GCC and the United States and to propose policy options for the United States to continue to derive maximum benefit from stable and reliable partnerships in the Gulf.

UNITED STATES-GULF COOPERATION COUNCIL SECURITY COOPERATION IN A MULTIPOLAR WORLD

INTRODUCTION

For the United States, the Arabian Gulf region remains one of the most geostrategically important locations in the world. Home to over half of the world's oil reserves and nearly a third of its natural gas,[1] the Gulf states continue to supply world markets with an important share of their energy supplies. Continuing to be one of the world's largest regional suppliers of energy and holding much of the world's spare capacity in crude oil production makes the region central to the stability of the global oil market.

The Gulf region also hosts one of the world's most important strategic choke points for global trade, the Straits of Hormuz, through which some 35 percent of global seaborne oil passes, in addition to natural gas and other trade goods.[2] The Gulf region's convenient location half-way between Europe and East Asia has given it further economic and strategic importance, with intensive cargo traffic passing through the sea passages of the region. The significance of the region is further increased because of its combined financial power in the form of savings and investment funds — which have grown steadily during the 2000s owing to high oil prices and revenues — that form an increasingly important element in U.S. international trade and investment interests.

The six member states of the Gulf Cooperation Council (GCC) — Bahrain, Kuwait, Oman, Qatar, Saudi Arabia, and the United Arab Emirates (UAE) — historically have been key U.S. partners in the region, helping secure regional stability while balancing out the ambitious political and economic interests of neighboring Iraq and Iran. For the GCC states, U.S. political and military support has been critical for their own defense, making the United States, for decades, the most influential external security partner for most GCC countries. The U.S. military has been deployed in, and has defended, the GCC states against regional military threats, including training local armed forces and providing a wide range of modern arms and defense systems to all six GCC members.

Changing geopolitical and economic realities both within and outside the region, however, have begun to change the nature of U.S.-GCC relations, and as a result, the GCC countries' geostrategic significance will likely raise the need for a reconsideration of the architecture of U.S.-GCC cooperation for the remainder of the 21st century. Regionally, the GCC economies today form the core center of economic and geopolitical power in the Gulf region, a status which has increased dramatically since the early-2000s with the removal of the Saddam regime in Iraq, and the increasing isolation of Iran in view of its controversial nuclear program and continuing destabilizing influence.

At the same time, several small GCC countries have begun to seek a greater role in international diplomatic circles, countering the long-held dominance of Saudi Arabia as the most significant regional political player and foreign investor. These efforts make more coordination on a supra-national GCC level more difficult, and will reinforce the need for the United States to engage bilaterally, but with a greater number of increasingly ambitious, and financially influential Gulf monarchies. The GCC states also show an increasing interest in diversifying their economic and security relations with other foreign partners, primarily China, India, and East Asia in general. This diversification of foreign relations poses a threat to intrinsic U.S. interests, but also offers a chance to include a greater number of countries in U.S.-forged security alliances.

Finally, the events of the Arab Spring beginning in 2010, which swept away several governments and have led to sustained political protest and civil unrest across the wider Middle East and North Africa, have impacted citizen-state relations in the region profoundly, including in the Arab Gulf monarchies. While most Gulf monarchies were spared Egypt-like political unrest owing to generous welfare states, Bahrain has faced a lengthy cycle of dissent and public protest which has confronted the United States with a considerable policy dilemma. One of the largest challenges for U.S. foreign policy toward the Gulf region will hence consist increasingly not in the "when" and "what" of direct military intervention, but in the "how" of bilateral cooperation to assist the region in eliminating the causes of political unrest that may in the future destabilize the region as a whole. These challenges grow principally from the region's economic issues, including those of increasing economic diversification and sustainable job creation; and from the need for good governance as a whole.

This monograph aims to review the likely challenges to the existing *modus operandi* of U.S.-GCC relations, and to suggest potential roads toward changing, yet maturing relations. This is done keeping in mind the other potentially constraining element in these relations, namely budgetary pressures in the U.S. and their impact on U.S. military strategies and priorities, which have raised concerns among GCC leaders about the future of U.S. security engagement in the region.

The monograph is organized as follows: Section 2 provides an overview of the historical evolution of the US-GCC security partnership during the 20th century; Section 3 explores the new factors that have changed the region's geopolitical architecture, challenging formerly established patterns in U.S.-GCC cooperation; and Section 4 discusses the implications for the shape of emerging relations over for the next decade.

THE HISTORICAL SYSTEM: FROM TRUCIAL STATES TOWARD THE MODERN GCC

U.S. relations with the GCC states date back many decades, having evolved in line with the wider Gulf's geopolitical shifts in regional power centers over time. Under the previous geopolitical configuration during and after World War II, the region was dominated by British interests, with *de facto* British protection for what were then called the "Trucial States," an alliance of those Gulf sheikhdoms that today make up the UAE, plus Bahrain and Qatar. Neighboring emirates such as Kuwait, the sultanate of Oman, and the monarchies of Bahrain and Saudi Arabia, were also Western allies relying to a greater or lesser extent on British protection against external and to some extent internal threats.[3]

Even prior to the discovery of oil in the region, the Gulf monarchies were strategically valuable allies owing to their pivotal location between Europe, Africa, and Asia. This offered British and allied trade and military vessels safe passage and naval facilities, and the Trucial coast also provided excellent and valuable harbor facilities to offload and transship merchandise aimed at the wider region and Central Asia, and to collect merchandise for European and Asian trade vessels.[4] This locational value further increased with the discovery of large oil deposits, first in Bahrain (1932), then Kuwait (1937), and Saudi Arabia (1938), at a time when the international shipping industry, including warships, was switching from coal to oil. The ensuing world war rendered secure oil supplies and bunkering locations decisive for military success.

The rapidly growing importance of oil production in the Arab Gulf monarchies accompanied similar oil production growth in neighboring Iran and Iraq, despite domestic political turmoil in those states. The attempted nationalization of Iran's oil industry in 1950 highlighted the vulnerability of these resources to domestic political change. Together with Iran and Iraq, the wider Gulf region increasingly assumed the role of the world's most important regional oil producer and reserve holder, holding more than half of the world's known oil reserves by the 1980s.[5] The Gulf as a region could only grow in importance as a potential strategic ally to all major post-war political blocs, and the Arab Gulf monarchies—due to their close historical ties with the British—soon evolved as the most reliable element in this system in its relations with Western allies.[6]

Thus with the end of World War II and the beginning of the Cold War, the Gulf states became a strategically important region both for Soviet and U.S. interests. Their role as growing producers of oil, and their geostrategic value at the pivot point between Europe, South East Asia, and Central Asia, all fueled competition between the United States and the Union of Soviet Socialist Republics (USSR).[7] From the earliest stages, Iran and Iraq formed an important part of the region's security system, both of them being populous and geographically large states with well-developed, semi-industrialized economies, as opposed to what were in the majority small, only recently evolved desert sheikhdoms with small landmasses, populations, and during the 1950s still overwhelmingly nonurban societies.[8]

Twin Pillar Politics: Saudi Arabia and Iran.

For this reason, among others, it was American interest in neighboring Iraq and Iran that initially defined U.S. relations with what would later evolve as the GCC states. A complex regional security system in the Gulf evolved during the 1950s, which involved three realistic competitors for regional political dominance. These were, first, Iran and Iraq, both states with long-established socio-political histories, strong economies increasingly dominated by their oil industries, and with the greatest share of the entire region's population of some 35.5 million by 1960; and second, Saudi Arabia, an Arab Gulf monarchy emerging as the region's largest oil producer.[9]

The role of Saudi Arabia vis-à-vis other Gulf monarchies at the time had to do with the Arabian Peninsula's geographic and economic make-up. Prior to the creation of the GCC in 1981, the Arab Gulf monarchies were a loose community of Gulf sheikhdoms and monarchies, which, except for Saudi Arabia, oversaw relatively small territories with populations not exceeding a few hundred thousand each. Economically, the discovery of large oil reserves in Saudi Arabia during the 1930s had begun to generate increasing revenue streams for the Saudi economy, with only Kuwait rivalling Saudi's wealth by the 1950s.[10] Similar oil discoveries in Abu Dhabi (part of today's UAE) and Oman were then another few years away, while Qatar's and Bahrain's modest reserves began to be developed to generate significant income only after the end of World War II and did not challenge Saudi Arabia's growing role as the region's largest oil producer, and hence the focal point of international political attention.

U.S. and British interests in particular focused on the hereditary monarchical systems of Saudi Arabia and, at the time, Iran, where the Shah (later ousted from power in 1979) promised both stable relations and, like Saudi Arabia, relied to a certain extent on military protection through his Western allies. During the 1960s, a **twin-pillar** policy became the key U.S. strategy in ensuring the stability of the Gulf's regional security system. Iran and Saudi Arabia, both regional emerging large powers, and both strongly allied to U.S. and Western governments, dominated the wider region, thus marginalizing any potentially threatening elements. Iranian-Saudi Arabian rivalry would also ensure that no one country would eventually end up significantly more powerful than the other, a fact which also corresponded to the intrinsic religious-sectarian differences between Sunni traditionalist Saudi Arabia, and Shiite (although, at the time secular-oriented) Iran.[11]

This regional system was not only to preserve regional security and stability over a long period, but also turned the Gulf into a bulwark against the advance of Communism and Soviet Russian interests that made increasing inroads into nearby South Asia. Reflecting this additional, ideological element in U.S. policy toward the wider region, the Richard Nixon Doctrine in 1969 incorporated the Gulf into American policymaking as a pivotal point for U.S. interests in the wider Middle East.

The Politics of "Dual Containment."

Nevertheless, evolving political developments in the region during the 1970s, and an escalation of regional Gulf tensions during the 1980s and 1990s, showed the limitations of the twin-pillar policy. The Arab oil embargos of 1973 and 1976, although of short duration, demonstrated to the Gulf states' Western allies that the economic and political tide could turn against Western markets that, by the 1970s, overwhelmingly depended on Gulf oil. The nationalization of wider Middle Eastern oil industries, including inside the Gulf region, had already begun to change the regional power dynamics between previously dominant Western corporations and the newly emerging national oil companies. This time also coincided with the gradual withdrawal of British forces from previous close cooperation with the Trucial Coast, leaving the Trucial States to become new, independent states, most of them to reunite in the UAE.[12]

After Iraq fell prey to domestic political turmoil under various military governments, Iran and Saudi Arabia remained as the politically and economically most powerful states in the region. But the Iranian revolution in 1979 resulted in the ousting of the Shah and his replacement by an Ayatollah-led theocratic Shiite state. This abruptly removed a key American ally and turned Iran from a former U.S. client to one of its fiercest enemies (Grand-Ayatollah Khomeini thereafter referring to the United States as the "Great Satan"). With the Soviet Union in mind, President Jimmy Carter stated that "An attempt by any outside force to gain control of the Gulf region will be regarded as an assault on the vital interests of the United States of America, and such an assault will be repelled by any means necessary, including military force"[13] — but in this context the President seemed to overlook the fact that the Gulf's most significant threat was no longer to be found in any "outside force"; its key security challenges since the 1980s arose entirely from its own, regional dynamics.

The war between Iran and Iraq during the 1980s cost more than one million lives over a period of 8 years, during which the entire Arabian Peninsula began to realize the destructiveness of regional political disputes, and the military threat which lay virtually at the doorsteps of even the West's close Gulf monarchy allies Saudi Arabia and Kuwait. The creation of the GCC marked the first visible reaction of the Gulf monarchies to these threats, even though the GCC's apparent long-term strategy consisted in economic rather than military cooperation. The aim was to create security through union rather than constructing yet another military opposition to the two raging Northern neighbors; while avoiding a union which would be politically and militarily dominated by its largest member state, Saudi Arabia.

The Iraqi invasion of Kuwait, followed by the first Gulf War in 1990-91, caused the full-scale escalation of regional military conflict, and removed any remaining doubts as to whether neighboring Iran, or neighboring Arab-Sunni-ruled Iraq, could be relied upon as guarantors of regional stability — or, indeed, as political allies of the Western powers. Of further heightened concern for the GCC states was their own, very limited military capability for self-defense. This was compensated for by the first active military engagement of U.S. forces in the conflict to defend not only Kuwait, but also neighboring Arab Gulf monarchies from the advance of Iraqi troops into Saudi Arabia. While this form of U.S. engagement in the region marked a climax in U.S.-GCC military relations, it also showed the utter failure of previously held security paradigms for the region resting on Iranian-Saudi supremacy.

U.S. policy under the Clinton administration moved from twin-pillar politics toward a policy of actively containing both Iraq and Iran, both of which were weakened militarily and economically from a decade of mutual war. Iraq also suffered heavily from its military defeat by U.S. and Coalition forces, despite the political survival of the Saddam regime. With the two northern neighbors significantly weakened, the GCC states emerged as the most important U.S. political allies through variously close bilateral relations with all of its member states.[14] U.S.-GCC military ties strengthened further as a result of the Gulf War. Several GCC states signed bilateral defense agreements with the United States, including Bahrain in 1991, Qatar in 1992, and the UAE in 1994. Access agreements for U.S. military forces followed, or were renegotiated to tie U.S. military troops stationed permanently in regional military bases, allowing for the training of local military forces in Saudi Arabia, Bahrain, and the UAE. Since the early-1990s, the GCC states have become a major military pillar for U.S. foreign policy not only in the Gulf region, but far beyond. For instance, the GCC states also provide much of the infrastructure and transit capability essential to U.S. missions in the wider region, including in Afghanistan.[15] U.S. military forces have access to key bases such as Al Dhafra Air Base in the UAE, Camp Arifjan in Kuwait, Al Udeid Air Base in Qatar, and the Naval Support Activity in Bahrain. Kuwait hosts as many as 15,000 U.S. troops; Qatar some 7,300; and the UAE some 3,000.[16] All GCC members are major staging hubs, operating training ranges, and offering logistical support for regional operations. Several GCC states also host U.S. Patriot missile batteries, such as Kuwait and the UAE.[17]

The GCC states have also emerged as premier markets for U.S. foreign military sales. Between 2007 and 2010, total U.S. weapons exports and defense services to the GCC states totaled over $26.7 billion, more than any other region in the world.[18] Reports for Fiscal Year 2011 include a fighter aircraft sale to Saudi Arabia worth some $29.4 billion, the single largest arms sale in American history,[19] rendering the GCC a formidable military client.

THE GULF'S CHANGING GEOPOLITICS DURING THE 2000s

The time since the early-2000s has dramatically re-shaped the geopolitical landscape of the Gulf, and in parallel U.S.-Gulf relations. The events of September 11, 2001 (9/11), when 19 armed Islamist terrorists hijacked four U.S. aircraft and flew them into New York City's World Trade Center's twin towers and the Pentagon in Washington, DC, demonstrated an emerging threat from within the Gulf region not only to the region itself, but to the United States as the main backer of its political systems. Of the 19 hijackers, 15 were Saudi citizens, the others coming from Egypt, Lebanon, and the UAE. They were born, raised, and allegedly radicalized in states which were considered key U.S. allies.[20]

While the event marked American relations with the wider Arab world for many years, it also precipitated a series of defining U.S. military interventions in and around the region, in the form of the U.S.-led invasion of Afghanistan, deposing the radical, theocratic-tribal Taliban regime under whose leadership al-Qaeda had been able to train at least some of the 9/11 hijackers; and in the case of the 2003 U.S. invasion of Iraq, deposing long-term President Saddam Hussein and his Baathist regime. Relations with some of the GCC states, Saudi Arabia in particular, were strained for a number of years by the strong Saudi element among the hijackers, allegedly radicalized inside Saudi mosques, while growing pressure within Saudi Arabia against U.S. "infidel" forces resulted in withdrawals of U.S. troops.

Iraq and the Surging Menace of Internal Conflict.

Undoubtedly one of the most important changes to the Gulf geopolitical landscape in the last 2 decades has been the aftermath of the 2003 U.S. invasion of Iraq. Once a Sunni regime and the main geopolitical competitor to both Iran and Saudi Arabia in the wider Gulf region, since 2003, Iraq has been characterized by a volatile political situation, insecurity, and a weak economy that can neither feed nor employ Iraq's young and mostly educated population. This leaves the government reliant almost entirely on oil export revenues for the running of the country. The country's oil sector itself has developed disappointingly, with no signs that Iraq, which holds the world's fifth largest oil reserves, can move its production capacity anywhere near its previously held targets. This means the prospects for Iraq to compete with neighboring Saudi Arabia in oil production seem remote at present, as are prospects for Iraq's presumably large but underexplored and underdeveloped gas reserves. This means that, despite resource potential, Iraq's hydrocarbon production remains of relatively little geopolitical consequence at present.

Iraq's volatile political situation has had far greater repercussions on the region as a whole. Political, sectarian, and ethnic struggles have characterized Iraq's political life since 2003, when U.S. forces first put in place a transitional government aimed at unifying the country.[21] Iraq's Shiite majority—economically and politically marginalized under the Sunni minority-based Saddam regime—has since gained political influence and constitutes the largest single sectarian voter bloc inside Iraqi politics, proving decisive for the election of current Iraqi Prime Minister Nouri al-Maliki. Reflecting the Saddam regime's former reliance on Sunnis, Iraq today more than ever has turned into a political battle field between rivalling Sunni-Shiite factions, which have become increasingly tied to the country's political system.[22] In parallel to the growing Sunni-Shiite split, Iraq's Kurds continue to live in a *de facto* separate Kurdish state, whose interactions with the central Iraqi government are complicated by the location of a large share of Iraq's oil and gas inside Kurdish territories.[23]

For the GCC states, the weakening of Iraq and political predominance of Shiite factions have deprived the Arab regimes in the Gulf of an important Sunni partner in their ideological and geostrategic competition with Iran. Iraq's continuingly unstable domestic political climate has given rise to a state of permanent insecurity, and daily clashes between sectarian groups, resulting in many thousands of dead Iraqis each year owing to terrorist attacks on homes, cars, hospitals, and even mosques; while Iraqi Kurdistan has drifted further away from the center owing to the continued violence between different sectarian branches of Iraq's Arabs.[24] Internationally operating terrorist organizations such as al-Qaeda have since found Iraq a fertile ground for new recruits and terrorist operations, exacerbating internal instability while posing a threat also to other countries, including the neighboring GCC states. It is Iraq's status as a source of domestic instability, the exacerbation of sectarian and ethnic conflict in a country so close to the GCC, coupled with the apparent inability of various allied forces such as U.S. troops and advisers to pacify Iraqi politics that have rendered Iraq a glaringly negative case study in the Gulf.

An even more problematic development seen in Iraq is the rise of domestic, regional menaces in the form of growing political instability, giving rise to increasingly radical forms of political Islamism, ethnic and sectarian tensions which also form an increasing part of wider Middle East political dynamics. Prolonged development of this kind could well render Iraq a very severe threat to regional security as a basis for radicalism to spread across the Gulf, and help revive long-held sectarian-political rivalries between Iran and Iraq on the one hand, and between Sunnis and Shiites across the Gulf countries themselves on the other. This means that in reality, the U.S. mission in Iraq is far from over, but also that it seems clear that purely military force engagement does not in itself resolve this situation. Here, too, a more systematic focus on institution-building and the application of intelligent mechanisms to encourage a strategic legislative solution to the continued deadlock between regions and their claim on Iraqi oil and gas resources may contribute significantly more to the solution of internal strife than continued reliance on military presence. In the GCC, too, sectarian and ethnic minorities exist, although to a lesser degree than in Iraq, with the exception of the largely disenfranchised expatriate population. However, the menace of escalating sectarian conflict within the GCC is real, particularly in Saudi Arabia and Bahrain, countries with somewhat larger Shiite populations; and the spillover of domestic turmoil from neighboring Iraq may yet constitute one of the most important threats to political stability in the GCC from within.

For the United States, this means most likely that future ways of engaging with the GCC to ensure domestic stability will need to entail more than mere military and technical means. They will include increasing cooperation in areas such as good governance, which is essential to strike the balance between domestic minorities so as to avert any outbreak of sectarian violence, as well as domestic political reform toward greater popular participation and government accountability; political transparency and fair media relations; and domestic economic reform, including the further diversification of the GCC economies toward more inclusive and sustained economic growth that offers employment opportunities for all GCC citizens. All of these goals form an intrinsic part of the interests of all GCC states, and the United States as a political and economic partner has an essential role to play.

Iran and the Politics of Nuclear Armament.

Of parallel significance, and with potential long-term consequences for the geopolitical situation of the wider Gulf region, has been the continuously worsening international confrontation over Iran's nuclear program. In pursuit of nuclear power for more than 40 years dating back to pre-Islamic Republic times, Iran has had a multi-decade history of nuclear controversy. U.S. doubts as to the possibility of a secret parallel nuclear weapons program have been voiced repeatedly since the mid-1970s, mainly based on U.S. intelligence reports.[25] Reports resurfaced in the 1980s during the Iran-Iraq war, and in the mid-1990s when U.S. intelligence stated that Iran was "aggressively pursuing a nuclear weapons capability and, if significant foreign assistance were provided, could produce a weapon by the end of the decade."[26] Iran has repeatedly stated that it intended to use its nuclear program for civilian purposes only.[27]

The current controversy surrounding Iran's nuclear program began to escalate in 2002, when an Iranian exile organization claimed that Iran had built nuclear facilities that had not been declared to nuclear inspectors sent to Iran by the International Atomic Energy Agency (IAEA) the year before. Some of the claims, which later proved unsubstantiated, triggered substantial international attention and prompted additional visits to relevant sites by IAEA inspectors. Their report concluded that Iran "had engaged in a variety of clandestine nuclear-related activities, some of which violated Iran's safeguards agreement" including plutonium separation experiments, uranium enrichment and conversion experiments, and importing various uranium compounds.[28] Subsequent agreements with the IAEA and the E3 countries (Britain, France, and Germany) resulted in the supposed suspension of enrichment activities, but the presidential election of Mahmoud Ahmadinajad in August 2005 involved a change of mind and the restatement of Iranian nuclear enrichment activities since then.[29]

Relations between Iran, the United States, and other international bodies such as the IAEA have since deteriorated continuously, and have triggered a series of gradually tightening sanctions to add to the existing sanctions arsenal the United States and some other Western nations have maintained against Iran since the mid-1980s. In June 2010 the U.S. Congress adopted the Comprehensive Iran Sanctions Accountability and Divestment Act of 2010 (CISADA) which substantially amends and extends the Iran Sanctions Act of 1996; in the same month, the United Nations Security Council (UNSC) adopted resolution 1929, the fourth in a series imposing sanctions on Iran. Further sanctions followed in November 2011 by the United States, and in July 2012 by the European Union (EU), targeting the export of Iranian oil with the aim of deterring Iran from further enrichment activities.[30]

The result has been an increasingly isolated Iran both politically, vis-à-vis most Western states and within the UNSC, and economically, particularly since 2012 with the implementation of oil-sector targeted sanctions. This is not to say that Iran has been struck as hard economically as the sanctions regime intended. While the Iranian government has been reported to have lost significant revenue streams particularly since the start of energy sector-related sanctions in mid-2013, various accounts suggest the country's economy is nowhere near a breaking point.[31] This is further evidenced by the continuation of Iranian oil exports to key Asian markets, including China, India, and South Korea, which have reduced but maintained their energy trade with Iran in spite of the sanctions. While the success of the current sanctions regime in convincing Iran to suspend its nuclear program is so far meager — if not counterproductive — the increasing sanctions regime has arguably contributed to Iran's growing political and economic isolation inside and outside the Gulf region.

For the GCC states, the Iranian question is not only a major geopolitical headache but also a severe threat to the region's long-term stability. Immediately, a nuclear-armed Iran in their immediate neighborhood offers reason for concern, even under what seems (despite the international sanctions regime) a de-escalating strategy by most Gulf states and the relatively slim possibility of a direct nuclear attack by Iran against GCC neighbors (which would probably also impact Iran itself owing to its geographic proximity). However, nuclear arms in Iran may lead to domestic calls within the GCC for reciprocal action in the form of a GCC-based nuclear arms program, and hence cause a nuclear arms race in the Gulf, which many regional observers see as potentially highly destabilizing.[32]

A regional nuclear arms race would leave the United States with no good policy options. If providing political or technological support, the United States would itself become a party to the race, fuelling a growing rift with Iran and reinforcing the latter's turn toward the alternative political spectrum ranging from Russia to China and North Korea. U.S. refusal to support GCC nuclear arms acquisitions, on the other hand, would spare America this scenario, but would likely create another rift between the United States and its GCC allies, which would themselves turn toward partners willing to supply the technology, thereby sidelining America as a key security partner. Both scenarios will hardly help strengthen rather than undermine regional stability in the longer term.

Perhaps of most immediate concern for the GCC states, however, is the geostrategic consequences of an armed escalation between outside forces, such as U.S. and Israeli strikes against Iran. The Iranian mainland is in immediate proximity to GCC neighbors UAE,

Qatar, and Bahrain, at its closest point merely some 40 kilometers away.[33] Both Iran and the GCC members share the Gulf as a main offshore oil and gas producing space, and the Straits of Hormuz as their main shipping route, through which close to 90 percent of all petroleum exported from the Gulf passes, including to key customers in Asia, Europe, and the United States.[34] Military attacks against Iran, even if directed against land-based infrastructure, would likely lock up the Straits of Hormuz for hydrocarbon transport for security reasons, as well as isolating a large part of the entire Gulf region's oil and gas production in the first place.

Iran itself has threatened multiple times to close the Straits of Hormuz if further sanctions are introduced or in the case of a military attack on the country, potentially by means of placing sub-sea mines across the Straits, stopping tanker traffic from the Gulf, which would target external oil markets but at the same time impact the GCC oil and gas exporters themselves. Even in the event of a time-limited military strike that would only involve the closure of the Straits for a couple of days, the economic short- and long-term consequences for Gulf hydrocarbon exports would be enormous in terms of monetary losses and political risk reassessments. The worst case scenario could result in a permanently weakened Iran enduring similar political chaos such as in neighboring Iraq, and creating a two-state instability problem at the doorstep of the Arab Gulf monarchies.

But the GCC states are also threatened by other Iranian weapons of influence, namely Iranian influence over Shiites living inside the GCC, with small but possibly disruptive minorities living in Saudi Arabia and the UAE, and a Shiite majority in Bahrain.

An internationally outlawed Iran, which responds by stirring domestic unrest via Shiite communities inside the GCC has been a long-term concern for many Gulf states, and may yet evolve as a major source of discontent between the two sides of the Gulf. All of these scenarios underline the enormous vulnerability of this small geographical area in case of any escalation of a conflict between Iran and outside players; and the difficulty for both the GCC and the United States as a key GCC ally in choosing the right strategy toward Iran.

A "Golden Age" of the GCC States? The Emergence of the GCC as an Economic Power Center.

Iran's political and economic isolation, however, has also held unexpected opportunities for the GCC. Together with Iraq's current political volatility, Iran's isolation largely eliminated two key regional players from the region's geo-economic sphere at the beginning of the 2010s. Rising oil prices since the early-2000s, contrasting with declining prices during the late-1980s and 1990s, provided the oil exporting Gulf monarchies with considerable windfall revenues of historical size, contributing to more than a decade of stable revenue rises, budgetary surpluses, and, in most cases, stable economic growth rates.[35] At the receiving end of this near-unprecedented revenue stream since the last oil price shock of the early-1980s, the GCC monarchies have weathered the trend for economic decline and political turmoil everywhere else across the Middle East during the 2010s (and during the late-2000s in Europe and North America).[36]

With the influence of two powerful neighbors attenuated on the Gulf's political and economic scene, this leaves the Gulf monarchies, collectively, as the region's by far most significant economic power center, not only in the Gulf but also in the economically weakened remaining wider Middle East. Their enormous oil revenues have also put the GCC monarchies into the fortuitous position of remaining the Gulf's only politically stable U.S. allies (political turmoil in Bahrain in 2012 taken aside), with growing political and economic influence beyond their own borders. The region's economic power has started to shift decisively from the region's former heavyweights, Iran and Iraq, toward the rising Gulf monarchies.

Important dynamic changes have also characterized the relationship of the GCC states with each other. While during the 1980s and 1990s, stagnant economic growth and mutual small-scale border disputes shaped GCC relations and hampered various shared projects, the time since the early-2000s has been characterized by considerably greater shared concerns, both external (Iraq, Iran) and internal (terrorism, Islamist radicals, Shiite-Sunni grievances, employment creation for nationals). The economic abundance induced by the 2000s oil revenue windfalls meant that considerable time and funds have been spent on economic diversification and employment-generating activities and generous welfare programs for GCC citizens. This mostly shared policy focus has rendered intra-GCC relations during the 2000s considerably less conflictive, and more harmonic, despite the maintenance of various, but mostly inconsequential political differences on international affairs issues.

A notable shift has also been taking place in the diversification of GCC economic and financial power away from formerly dominant Saudi Arabia toward various centers of economic power and interest also in the GCC's smaller member states. With populations of just a few million each, some of the GCC's small monarchies—Qatar, the UAE, and Kuwait—have found themselves among the world's wealthiest countries on a per capita basis. Storming ahead with post-modern skylines, and rapidly growing nonoil sectors such as tourism, culture, real estate, and finance, many GCC members are now economic political brands in their own right, ranging from Dubai's metropolism to Qatar's knowledge cities. Many GCC states' oil wealth has also translated into extensive interests in external economic and political engagement, beyond Saudi Arabia.

The GCC states' strengthened economic position in several cases has also been tied to rising geopolitical ambitions by its smaller members, contrary to the past when such ambitions had been largely limited to Saudi Arabia. Qatar and the UAE have emerged as diplomatic centers in their own right, entertaining interests in foreign politics and mediating roles, in addition to a growing number of high-profile domestic projects including Qatar securing the games for the 2022 football World Cup. Qatar has diplomatically been involved in a number of outside conflicts, playing roles in Tunisia, Egypt, Libya, and Syria.[37] *Al-Jazeera*, Qatar's news channel, now assumes an important role in the cross-Arab media landscape, participating briskly—and not impartially—in political debates, including in the context of Egypt's 2011 revolution and the 2013 ousting of the country's Muslim Brotherhood-led government.[38] Qatar and Saudi Arabia have not shied away from becoming agents of political change such as in Egypt and Syria, engaging directly via financial and media support for elements within the political process.[39] The UAE, on the other hand, sent their own troops to Afghanistan in 2003 and pledge to keep troops deployed after the withdrawal of international forces in 2014, supported rebels in Libya and Syria and the GCC-brokered power change in Yemen, and have become a key U.S. partner in implementing significant economic and political sanctions against Iran.[40] Significantly, the UAE has bought the most sophisticated missile defense system sold by the United States as part of the country's efforts in assembling a regional defense system against Iran.[41] With plans for four nuclear power reactors by 2020, the UAE will further host GCC's and the Arab world's first civilian nuclear program, relying on Korean and U.S. technology partners as well as long-term U.S. political support.[42]

GCC financial power is now not only tangible in the region, but beyond in the form of direct investments and acquisitions made by the GCC multiple investment funds and their older brothers, the GCC states' Sovereign Wealth Funds (SWFs). The sheer scale of these funds is unprecedented. A 2013 KPMG study estimates the value of the Kuwait Investment Authority at U.S.$296 billion; Saudi Arabia's Monetary Agency (SAMA) foreign holdings at U.S.$533 billion; and Abu Dhabi Investment Authority at U.S.$627 billion.[43] A 2013 UN estimate suggests wealth accumulated by GCC SWFs could have reached U.S.$1.8 trillion, or around a third of assets accumulated by SWFs worldwide.[44] Their investments are increasingly global in a range of sectors such as mines, infrastructure, agriculture, and industries.

On the other hand, a rising number of requests by international organizations, including most recently the International Monetary Fund (IMF), for the GCC economies to contribute a rising share into economic rebuilding packages for Europe and North America show by now the inevitable economic significance of the GCC economies for the functioning of the U.S. economy. The GCC economies' influence extends to their role in upholding U.S. capital markets through their vast assets, which continue to be held over-whelmingly in U.S. dollars. Having lost more than 20 percent of their asset value during the financial crisis of 2008-09, the GCC economies have been just as de-pendent on U.S. fiscal stability as the U.S. market is to GCC asset strength, for any systematic disinvest-ment of GCC capital assets held in U.S. dollars toward alternative markets in Asia and Africa, and shifts in currency preferences, would have significant effects on the value of the U.S. dollar.[45] This growing finan-cial interdependence is a new development, and one unlikely to reverse over the next decade in view of the continued importance of oil exports for the GCC econ-omies—priced overwhelmingly in U.S. dollars—and the U.S. market's continued need for foreign invest-ment to finance its growing fiscal deficits.

Investment relations are mirrored by the increas-ing significance to the region of U.S. trade in commod-ities. Total two-way trade between the United States and the GCC states in 2011 totaled over U.S.$100 billion, turning the GCC into currently the 10th larg-est U.S. export market, a position reflected by a new framework agreement between the United States and the GCC signed in September 2012 to expand trade and strengthen economic ties with each other.[46]

Growing Influence of Asia.

The United States is no longer the GCC's only, nei-ther its most important, trade and investment partner. Asian economies now account for a rising share in Gulf trade, both as an export destination for Gulf oil and natural gas, and as a technology partner and the origin of much of the GCC's food and other merchandise imports. This shift in GCC market orientation largely reflects the rise in Asian economic power.[47] Asian economies are expected to account for a vast share in global energy demand growth well into the 2030s, contrasting with declining growth in demand for conventional fossil fuels in the former key markets, Europe and North America.[48] The latter's expected oil and gas self-sufficiency by 2020 further reduces the weight of the U.S. energy market for GCC decisionmaking, shifting the focus instead toward those markets where most growth is expected: Asia.

Already today, Asian markets account for approximately 40 percent of global energy consumption, and a rapidly rising share of GCC oil and gas production. Asia receives over 50 percent of Saudi Arabia's crude oil exports in addition to nearly all of its refined products exports; while over 90 percent of crude oil exports by the UAE, Kuwait, and Qatar go to Asia.[49] The market for GCC exports in liquefied natural gas—coming from Qatar, Abu Dhabi, and Oman—is even more concentrated, where above 95 percent of all exports go to Asia—most of them under long-term contracts with durations of 15 to 20 years.[50]

The importance of Asian economies for individual GCC trade relations outperforms that of traditional trade partners Europe and North America. China alone accounted for over 10 percent of total GCC trade in 2011, surpassed only by India with 11 percent; while the combined share in trade volume between the GCC and the U.S./EU declined from around 40 percent at the beginning of the 1990s, to merely 20 percent in 2011.[51] While strong U.S.-Saudi trade relations and the weight of Saudi Arabia within the GCC market still maintain a critical U.S. role as an important overall GCC trade partner, for many of the GCC's smaller economies the most significant trade relations are now dominated by Asian economies, with a declining role for U.S. trade (see Table 1). With the onset of the financial crisis that struck the United States and Europe in 2008, additional impetus has been given to those GCC market analysts who have seen the future of GCC energy trade and financial investment increasingly shifting toward Asia.[52]

Country	Trading Partners (Percent of Foreign Trade)
Saudi Arabia	1° EU27 (15.2%), 2° United States (13.1%), 3° China (12.8%)
Bahrain	1° Saudi Arabia (8.9%), 2° EU27 (6.7%), 3° United States (4.4%), 4° India (3.1%), 5° Japan (3%)
United Arab Emirates	1° India (17.8%), 2° EU27 (12.3%), 3° Japan (10.1%)
Kuwait	1° South Korea (14%), 2° Japan (13.9%), 3° India (12.8%), 4° EU27 (11.3%), 5° United States (10.4%), 6° China (10.4%)
Qatar	1° Japan (24.4%), 2° EU27 (18.7%), 3° South Korea (13.2%), 4° India (7%), 5° Singapore (6.1%), 6° United States (4.6%), 7° China (3.7%)
Oman	1° China (19%)

Source: A. Molavi, "'The New Silk Road', 'Chindia', and the Geo-Economic Ties that bind the Middle East and Asia," B. Wakefield, S. L. Levenstein, eds., *China and the Gulf*, Washington, DC: Woodrow Wilson International Center for Scholars, 2011.

Table 1. Main Trade Partners of the GCC States, 2010.

In turn, Asian investors are keen to access GCC markets for a variety of their goods, ranging from food and household commodities, to high technology and, increasingly, direct investment into the GCC countries' energy sectors themselves. This interest stems from the by now high dependence of many East Asian economies on Middle East and GCC hydrocarbon exports: Oil from the GCC economies and Iran account for over 85 percent of Japanese and South Korean crude oil imports (Japan being the world's third largest net consumer), while nearly a quarter of Chinese oil imports is covered by just three countries, Saudi Arabia, Kuwait, and the UAE. GCC exporters supply more than a quarter of Japanese and Korean liquefied natural gas (LNG), and around a fifth of Chinese LNG supplies.[53]

Unsurprisingly, Asian national oil companies (NOCs) have shown increasing interest in GCC oil and gas production, where Chinese, Japanese, and South Korean companies have since the early-2000s dramatically raised their presence.[54] Asian companies have secured highly sensitive technology-based agreements, most significantly through selection of a Korean partner to set up the UAE's nuclear program, which includes four reactors by 2020, introducing civilian nuclear power to the region outside Iran.[55] Asian companies also dominate other energy market sub-segments, such as the growing GCC-based renewables sector through sales and technology transfer of solar technology, in which Chinese companies are now world leaders.[56]

While much of the visible relations between the GCC and Asian countries are concentrated around economic issues, there is a realistic chance that such relations may turn at any point of time in the future into full-fledged security relations that are likely increasingly to rival those between individual GCC states and the United States. Increasingly frequent high-level state visits and a growing number of mutual cooperation agreements, loans, gifts, and more, all of which have intensified throughout the 2000s and 2010s, show an obvious desire on both sides to maintain close ties. Although no direct military agreements are publicly known and do not necessarily follow from visits of this kind, Asian partners in principle offer alternative sources for military training, as well as weapons exports.[57] The firm plans of the UAE and Saudi Arabia to develop indigenous defense industries, as part of their security strategy and economic diversification plans, could lead both countries to seek technology and expertise transfers from Asian partners. For instance, in the UAE, Tawazun is the government's main investment vehicle to achieve the country's defense industry ambitions. Over recent years, Tawazun has established strategic partnerships with several international defense and security firms.[58]

Evaporating Alliances? US-GCC Relations and the "Arab Spring."

The political turmoil that has swept across the Middle East and North Africa since the end of 2010, popularly known as the "Arab Spring," was an unexpected test to U.S.-GCC relations. Popular protest removed from power the long-term regimes of Ben Ali in Tunisia (January 2010), Hosni Mubarak in Egypt (January 2011) and Muammar Gaddhafi in Libya (October 2011). Protests also led to a GCC-brokered handover of power by Yemen's president for more than 30 years, Ali Abdallah Saleh, in February 2012;

the outbreak of *de facto* civil war in Syria between Syrian President Bashar Asad's regime and opposition forces in 2012; and the eventual removal of Mohamed Morsi's Muslim Brotherhood-led government in Egypt in July 2013. The events since 2010 mark a dramatic shift in political power in the Arab world, removing both long-term dictators and, in the cases of Tunisia's Ali and Egypt's Mubarak, long-held political allies both of America and the GCC.

The Arab Spring has affected different GCC members in different ways, with some shared opportunities and concerns. The ousting of long-established political regimes in many of the Arab world's republics removed political friends and foes of GCC states alike. The Mubarak regime in Egypt, largely seen as a key political ally for both the United States and most of the GCC states, stood for more than 2 decades for the stability of one of the Arab world's political and cultural core centers, particularly after the political disintegration of rivalling Iraq; while some regime changes, such as the removal of the long-isolated Gaddhafi regime in Libya and the ongoing struggle against the Alawite Asad regime in Syria are widely seen as a welcome, even if not applauded, development for most GCC states. Qatar, by contrast, has seemed to support the downfall of the Mubarak regime and supported the subsequent Muslim Brotherhood-led government—a notably contrasting political stance to neighboring Saudi Arabia.

The Arab Spring has arguably repositioned the GCC monarchies vis-à-vis the rest of the Arab world. Facing a largely unstable Arab world in which many republics have been on the brink of political and economic collapse, the Arab Gulf monarchies have been largely spared from political uproar, in large part thanks to their enormous economic wealth and a decade-long track record of comparably generous welfare states and employment-oriented economic growth policies. Bahrain taken aside, the Arab Spring has left the GCC states in the paradoxical position of having become the Arab world's last remaining bulwark against political protest, a status shared with the two other remaining Arab monarchies, Morocco and Jordan. Geopolitically, the GCC as a region has gained significantly since the early-2011s owing to the effective removal of previous alternative economic and political power centers in the Middle East: most importantly Egypt—now politically torn by post-revolutionary domestic struggles and decreasing oil and gas exports; and Syria—torn by domestic political conflict resembling ever more closely an evolving long-term civil war. With Iraq weakened and Iran isolated politically and economically, this leaves the GCC with its growing oil wealth as something of a "last region standing," displaying a remarkable resilience to the otherwise region-wide raging Arab Spring.

At the same time, the perceived U.S. abandonment of the Mubarak regime, a shared key ally of the GCC and Egypt, sent important signals to the GCC about the potential durability of U.S. political and military support in the event of popular demand for more democratic rights and access to their country's economic resources. This intrinsic U.S. dilemma in the region has since further risen in the aftermath of the events in Bahrain in early-2011, when for the first time significant protest waves began to hit a Gulf monarchy, and one most vulnerable to protest owing to preexisting sectarian cleavages between the Sunni royal family and the majority Shiite Bahraini population.

In February and March 2011, Bahrain experienced unprecedented peaceful mass protests, which were met by brutal repression, resulting in more than 30 dead (mostly protesters or bystanders), jail sentences for prominent opposition leaders as well as, in subsequent months, bloggers, journalists, and others expressing political dissent with the government; and severe infrastructure and economic damage in the aftermath of the protests.[59] Subsequent months were characterized by smaller-scale protest but entailed more seriously a growing polarization of Bahrain's society along sectarian lines. Saudi Arabia, Bahrain's most important regional ally, was reportedly involved in the military reaction and clampdown of initial protests, alarmed by the prospect of protests similar to those in Egypt and Tunisia reaching the GCC states and the additional complications associated with the existing Sunni-Shiite split in Bahrain.[60]

The United States was faced with a formidable political dilemma; long-term support to protect Bahrain's security and stability had been assured by successive U.S. governments and had stood at the core of U.S. security support for the entire GCC region. Bahrain hosts the U.S. Fifth Fleet, and the Bahraini army has received U.S. military training. The events of February 2011 left U.S. forces literally watching from the front row the evolving escalation of domestic Bahraini politics between different sectarian fronts (a scenario more than anything else seen as the ultimate red line for multiple GCC governments), protestors calling for more democracy, greater governmental transparency and jobs, all of this merely a few kilometers away from neighboring Qatar and the UAE. The alleged involvement of Iran further charged the political situation and demonstrated the fine line between democratic protest and the escalation of protest into sectarian struggle, involving not only nationals but foreign intervention.

Protest in favor of democratic reform, however, and the Bahraini government's subsequent reactions in brutally repressing protest and imprisoning opposition politicians, also resulted in mounting pressure by human rights groups and democracy supporters in the United States for it to step up its stance against the Bahraini government.[61] The perceived U.S. role as a bystander to conflict rang alarm bells in and around Bahrain; would similar protests in the future, and their potential escalation, again entail a passive American role? Will U.S. allies stand by GCC governments in the case of systematic imprisonment of political opponents to Egyptian or Tunisian dimensions? Will U.S. support for human rights and democratic movements lead to a change of heart by U.S. policymakers against former ally governments in the GCC?

LESSONS AND OPTIONS FOR U.S. POLICY TOWARD THE GCC

The Gulf region's changing overall security system, tied to the continuing instability of Iraq, the threat of an evolving nuclear Iran, and an economically rising GCC (including beyond the GCC's formerly dominant economic player, Saudi Arabia) has meant that the U.S. role as a political and military partner has been similarly changing and is likely to continue to evolve. "Twin pillar" politics and the policy of "dual containment" seem both to have failed in offering the region stability, while the limitations of U.S. political strategy not only in the Gulf region, but indeed the wider Middle East, in providing security for the United States itself were demonstrated by the 9/11 attacks.

At the same time as these profound challenges await strategists both in the United States and the GCC states themselves, the United States as a military partner has been changing as well. The enduring Iraq debacle, which has resulted in yet another unstable state at the heart of the Middle East and in immediate proximity to the GCC, has left many former supporters of U.S. engagement in the region disappointed and cynical. The large financial and human cost of U.S. military engagement in the region appears to have worn out support among different political groups within U.S. policy circles which was previously consistent for decades; while the onset of North America's and Europe's most profound financial crisis for many decades in 2008 has meant that financial means for U.S. military interventions has been reduced significantly. The ongoing U.S. defense budget adjustments have raised concerns among the GCC leaders about the future of U.S. military capabilities, and U.S. willingness and ability to engage in the region. Although the U.S. Government reaffirmed in a strategic military document in 2011 its commitment to assuring the security and stability of the Middle East, the GCC countries remain worried about the future.[62]

This raises questions as to the future shape of U.S. security cooperation in the region, which has from the beginning been a cornerstone of U.S.-Gulf relations. In what follows we suggest those cornerstones that may form part of a future U.S.-GCC relationship in view of all these developments.

From Militant Unilateralism Toward Candid Multilateralism.

The past decade has demonstrated like no other time that the United States is no longer alone in the Gulf. Several European countries are strengthening their positions as the GCC's strategic partners. French involvement in the region, after setting up a military base in Abu Dhabi in 2009,[63] is likely to increase in the future, particularly after listing the stability in the Gulf region as one of the French government's top priorities.[64] The current United Kingdom (UK) government is keen to strengthen its presence in the region and reforge strategic alliances with all GCC countries.[65] Growing Asian interests in line with growing Asian energy needs and increasing dependence on Gulf oil and gas has resulted in a multitude of new, politically and economically significant partners for the GCC members. In the economic sphere, Asian companies, both private and state-backed, now compete increasingly with U.S. and partner companies over market access, with particular significance in the case of company access to the oil and gas sectors. Continued Asian engagement with sanctioned Iran further implies growing Asian influence in those neighboring countries that American diplomacy no longer reaches. In view of this, the importance of Asian intermediaries and of Asian ties to both sides of the Gulf is likely only to increase over the coming years, and American foreign policy will need to come to terms with this reality in as a constructive way as possible.

The United States will likely face a Gulf region whose interest in more diversified security partners will entail a role for Asian countries, including through weapons purchases and the transfer of sensitive technology, including nuclear. The space for U.S. engagement nevertheless remains large, particularly in view of the long-established historical ties between U.S. and GCC militaries, and the continued stationing of U.S. forces and ships at the coasts of several GCC partners. It would seem unlikely that any of the GCC states would wish to invite the military presence of various different foreign partners, thus rendering a stable U.S. presence in the Gulf a likely continuing pillar of GCC-U.S. relations. A U.S. strategy that continues to ensure the durability of this presence appears advisable in this context as long as GCC partners wish for such; while the financially strong position of many GCC states would arguably allow for new arrangements over the financial burden-sharing of such presence that would alleviate pressure on the U.S. side in view of current budgetary constraints.

Not only foreign security partners have changed; the United States faces an increasingly self-confident array of wealthy Gulf monarchies whose economic power and political ambition has made the GCC a group of states that no longer is simply on the receiving end of U.S. military assistance in return for security of oil supplies. Many GCC nations aspire to acquire strategic ways of thinking, rather than primarily foreign technology and military protection, to pursue their own security strategies along with their own diplomatic efforts in the wider Middle East as part of a new self-understanding following their own, regional political ideals. The heterogeneity of the GCC states is nowhere more visible than in the partly opposing political standpoints between Saudi Arabia — with a more traditional outlook and strategy — and Qatar, described as a country whose foreign policy successes constitute a "'branding' strategy that seeks to showcase Qatar as uniquely able to influence Arab and regional politics, well above what might be expected based on its relatively small size."[66]

Accommodating the emerging geopolitical ambitions of several GCC member states may at first pose a greater challenge to regional security cooperation than to relations with the United States itself. With several keen new international actors, particularly Qatar, but also member states with more individualist policies such as Oman, the main challenge will undoubtedly consist in generating consent for closer political and economic coordination at the GCC level. Declining support for a common currency is perhaps one of the most illustrative examples of what appears to be a mounting lack of interest by many GCC members in cooperating at the economic and political level. This situation calls for a U.S. role that could be supportive of cross-regional cooperative efforts, particularly in view of the challenges that are shared by all GCC states in the form of domestic dissent and sectarian tensions.

On the other hand, individual GCC states' key interests in other Arab countries, such as Egypt, Tunisia, Yemen, Syria, and Lebanon, mean that a security partnership between the United States and the GCC states may increasingly entail an element of foreign policy in proxy countries. This picture is complicated by variously different, sometimes opposing foreign policy views by different GCC states, with differing views by Qatar and Saudi Arabia on Egypt being a prime example. Nevertheless, it is sensible to remember that any of the regimes that have fallen, or may yet fall prey to the political turmoil of the Arab Spring, may be a client, friend, or foe of GCC states; and that U.S. policy in these countries will likely affect the security relationship with the GCC states themselves.

This is a situation of no first best policy option—political realism would dictate a U.S. foreign policy toward the region that carefully weighs between ideological and pragmatic political standpoints. However, if anything, this problem set suggests an important role for communication between U.S. and GCC security partners in a proactive manner. It reflects possibly what Fawaz A. Gerges ascribes to the first Barack Obama administration's Middle East policy:

> Obama seized on the desire evident both in the United States and across the world to see America move away from militant unilateralism and return to the traditional multilateralism in international affairs that had steered the nation through the first decade following the end of the Cold War. . . . Now more than ever, [President Obama] said, diplomacy and engagement are critical to rebuilding 'our alliances, repairing our relationships around the world, and actually making us more safe in the long term'.[67]

The Limits of a Unitary Strategy.

The Bahrain uprisings nevertheless have illustrated a particular policy dilemma in the Gulf: whether or not U.S. security cooperation should entail the unconditional support of political regimes in the GCC irrespective of their domestic actions. Human rights and the support of democratic movements form an essential part of American self-understanding, and while the GCC monarchies have never been considered formal democracies (as was Iran's Shah regime or Egypt's Mubarak regime for instance), the events in Bahrain in 2011 re-raised the question of how far U.S. support in such a case would go. Would U.S. forces support the Bahraini government or other GCC governments in a similar position over the long term? Would U.S. democracy movements take sides with protesters? Would U.S. inaction allow one GCC state to fall into chaos, potentially in favor of protest movements but with the consequence of potentially destabilizing other GCC states?

The answer to such questions will likely become an important element in the evolving security relationship between the United States and the GCC states. It may entail a much more pluralistic U.S. policy among the GCC states, or one in which a strengthened GCC institution itself redefines its responses to mutually shared domestic threats. A sensible U.S. policy response will also entail a greater role for providing training in "soft" military strategies, such as the use of intelligence and strategic communication by domestic governments to respond to, but also listen to domestic sources of discontent. Such strategic tools once again highlight the continued importance of U.S. and European security partners in the region owing to their considerable experience with such nontraditional security tools.

Security Cooperation and the Use of Unconventional Tools.

Not only in the Bahraini context, the GCC states' increasing geopolitical weight, and their own structural advantages and challenges mean the nature of threats to their national security has been transformed tremendously, to include a myriad of unconventional menaces such as domestic economic and political unrest, sectarian tensions, and the side effects of looming conflict in neighboring countries. From the U.S. perspective particularly, political pro-democracy movements inside the Gulf countries make it clear that conventional military strategy alone will not be able to help. All of these challenges require a very different arsenal of policy and security responses, away from heavy artillery and missiles toward domestic dialogue, inclusive political responses to real economic grievances, and an improved level of communication between governments and their citizens.[68]

U.S. cooperation with the GCC states may benefit from more weight being placed on those intangible security assets such as intelligence and communication that enable states not only to engage in traditional situations of warfare, but in countering domestically induced conflict and political uprisings. Several GCC countries are keen to develop their own unmanned aerial vehicle capabilities, to be used for purposes ranging from surveillance to offensive operations. Political level exchange, but also research cooperation and communication via shared forums and institutions over a variety of domestic security-sensitive topics may form part of this, most importantly encouraging domestic reform in the economic and political spheres. Obama's comments on wider U.S. foreign policy and engagement with foreign partners may entail this in a basic message:

> Recall that earlier generations faced down fascism and communism not just with missiles and tanks, but with sturdy alliances and enduring convictions. They understood that our power alone cannot protect us, nor does it entitle us to do as we please.[69]

Moreover, any U.S. security strategy in the wider Gulf region will need to pay growing attention toward efforts that focus on other areas of GCC economic stability. They should help GCC governments plan and carry through necessary economic reforms, maintain an open, trade-conducive domestic climate and support the GCC economies in diversifying their domestic industries and private sector development to help foster self-sustained economic growth and employment as the basis for GCC domestic stability. U.S. security interests and the growing interdependence between GCC and U.S. capital markets also imply an important role for the management of U.S. capital resources, and fiscal and dollar stability, to counteract growing concerns in the GCC over the stability of the dollar, and hence of its strategic financial assets.

Regional challenges, the outlook for economic decline should oil prices decline over a sustained period of time, and rising regional economic grievances or sectarian tensions all pose important challenges to the GCC states and demand long-sighted policy responses. An increasingly important U.S. role could thus involve mediating and forging such continued cooperative efforts, including in the area of pressing economic reform that could best be dealt with at a regional level. Engaging here entails a growing diplomatic, rather than U.S. military role, and will require delicate skills to avoid any sort of economic-ideological "interference," and may involve the dissemination of research and cooperative work in addition to plain policy assistance.

Time for New Regional Security Arrangements?

There is an argument that security in the Gulf region would be best served by a regionalized security forum in the shape of a strengthened GCC that further reinforces mutual security sector cooperation, or in the shape of a wider regional Gulf forum that includes other non-GCC member states as well. One suggested mechanism includes a Helsinki-style security forum, with the aim of developing regional conflict resolution mechanisms and of reducing regional tensions.[70] Such a forum could include the GCC members as well as Iraq, Iran, and Yemen, under an organizational umbrella not very different from that of the Association of Southeast Asian Nations (ASEAN) Regional Forum (ARF), but with greater focus on military and security cooperation than in the ASEAN context.

Yet, taking into account the current and enshrined animosities between Iran and a few GCC countries, this suggested forum may be unrealistic, and in any case is far from being materialized in the foreseeable future. On the one hand, Iranian assertive diplomatic and security postures in the Middle East worry the GCC countries. On the other, the presence of U.S. military forces in the Gulf region only increases Iran's threat perception. The likelihood of Saudi Arabia and Iran working together remains remote. Previous rapprochement attempts between Saudi and Iran have failed to ease their tensions. Both countries, with opposing ideologies, have been competing for influence in the region and have engaged in many proxy wars.

However, what is realistic is to create a regional security entity that groups the GCC countries with their strategic Western partners, namely the United States, the UK, and France. Such a forum could entail regular meetings to discuss regional security matters, and to foster cooperative efforts such as shared military and security training. It would help in reconciling views on security and foreign policy matters of common interest, as well as increasing the efficiency of use of all the resources available to stabilize the region.

CONCLUSION

The profound changes in regional geopolitical dynamics in the Gulf since the early-2000s render the region a highly challenging environment for U.S. foreign policy. Still the world's single most important producer region of oil, the Gulf states remain a region of essential economic and political interest for the United States. The GCC economies form the most important, and so far most stable block of countries within the region that have consistently been tied to their U.S. partnership, despite disagreements and variously fluctuating relations between individual GCC states and the United States. The geopolitical weight of the GCC states at a time of continuing domestic instability in Iraq, and an increasingly isolated Iran, has risen dramatically over the past 10 years; the GCC states' enormous economic power, coupled to some of the most stable political states in the entire Middle East and North Africa region, call for continuously close U.S.-GCC relations in the security sphere, as well as in terms of financial investment and trade as an important element in U.S. foreign policy.

The 2000s saw the rise of internal radical trends, drawn across religious and sectarian lines within the Gulf region, and of the growing confrontation with nuclear Iran in parallel with the political eclipse of turbulent Iraq. At the same time, smaller GCC states increased in economic power and escaped the shadow of Iran, Iraq, and Saudi Arabia as the dominant geopolitical players. In this context, the nature of U.S.-GCC security relations may well evolve to include a range of different policy instruments, other than traditional forms of cooperation through direct military protection and training, and the sale of U.S. weapons to the GCC states. These should increasingly involve cooperation and training in areas such as formal intelligence, media, and communication management, including strategic communication to ameliorate rather than exacerbate potential domestic conflict as a threat to all Gulf monarchies alike. It may also involve a more frequent exchange over wider education and training methods, and research enabling the GCC states to diversify further their economies and to create lasting and inclusive wealth reaching all parts of their populations. For while in the past U.S.-GCC security relations have often been reduced to outright military protection, it has been the 2000s that have marked the growing importance of the idea that for the United States, losing hearts and minds in the wider Arab region constitutes a threat to national security at home. For this reason, it is to be hoped that U.S.-GCC relations by the 2020s will look very different from today.

ENDNOTES

1. *International Energy Statistics*, Energy Information Administration (EIA), 2013, available from *www.eia.gov/cfapps/ipdbproject/IEDIndex3.cfm*.

2. "World Oil Transit Checkpoints," EIA, 2013, available from *www.eia.gov/countries/regions-topics2.cfm?fips=WOTC*.

3. For a detailed history, see J. Crystal, *Oil and Politics in the Gulf: Rulers and Merchants in Kuwait and Qatar*, Cambridge, UK: Cambridge University Press, 1995; Rosemarie Said Zahlan, *The Making of the Modern Gulf States: Kuwait, Bahrain, Qatar, the United Arab Emirates, and Oman*, Reading, UK: Ithaca Press, 1998; Frauke Heard-Bey, *From Trucial States to United Arab Emirates: A Society in Transition*, London, UK: Motivate, 2005.

4. Crystal; Heard-Bey.

5. EIA, *International Energy Statistics.*

6. James Onley, "Britain and the Gulf Shaikhdoms, 1820-1971: The Politics of Protection," *Occasional Paper*, No. 4, Washington, DC: Center for International and Regional Studies, Georgetown University School of Foreign Service in Qatar, 2009, available from *repository.library.georgetown.edu/bitstream/handle/10822/558294/ CIRSOccasionalPaper4JamesOnley2009.pdf?sequence=5.*

7. Robert John Schneller, *Anchor of Resolve: A History of the U.S. Naval Forces Central Command/Fifth Fleet*, Washington, DC: Naval Historical Center, Department of the Navy, 2007; Martin Indyk, "U.S. Policy Priorities in the Gulf: Challenges and Choices," *International Interests in the Gulf Region*, Abu Dhabi, UAE: Emirates Center for Strategic Studies and Research, 2004, p. 2.

8. Crystal; Heard-Bey.

9. The population of the Gulf region, including Iran and Iraq by 1960 stood at 34.4 million, of which Iran had a population of almost 22 million; Iraq 7.3 million; and Saudi Arabia, 4 million, compared with less than a million inhabitants in all other Gulf sheikhdoms. *World Development Indicators*, Washington, DC: World Bank, 2013, available from *data.worldbank.org/data-catalog/ world-development-indicators.*

10. Tim Niblock, ed., *State, Society, and Economy in Saudi Arabia*, Abingdon, UK: Taylor & Francis, 1982.

11. *The Gulf Security Architecture: Partnership with the Gulf Cooperation Council*, A Majority Staff Report prepared for the use of the Committee on Foreign Relations, U.S. Senate, 112th Congress, 2nd Session, Washington, DC: U.S. Congress, June 19, 2012, pp. 7-8; Indyk.

12. The United Arab Emirates are a federation of the seven emirates: Abu Dhabi, Ajman, Dubai, Fujairah, Ras Al-Khaimah, Sharjah, and Umm Al-Quwain.

13. Jimmy Carter, "The State of the Union Address Delivered before a Joint Session of the Congress, January 23, 1980," *The American Presidency Project*, Santa Barbara, CA: University

of California, available from *www.presidency.ucsb.edu/ws/index. php?pid=33079#axzz1spb4HZYc*.

14. Indyk.

15. U.S. Congress, p. 19.

16. *Ibid.*, pp. 12, 15, 17.

17. *Ibid.*

18. Paul Kerr, based on numbers from *Foreign Military Sales, Foreign Military Construction Sales and Other Security Cooperation, Historical Facts as of 30 September 2010*, Washington, DC: Department of Defense, Defense Security Cooperation Agency, 2012, p. 28, available from *www.dsca.mil/programs/biz-ops/factsbook/ FiscalYearSeries-2010.pdf,* and *www.sipri.org/research/armaments/ transfers/transparency/national_reports/united_states/us_ dscafacts_2010.pdf.*

19. "2011, Special Joint Press Briefing on U.S. Arms Sales to Saudi Arabia," Press Release, U.S. Department of State, December 29, 2011, available from *www.state.gov/r/pa/prs/ps/2011/12/ 179777.htm.*

20. National Commission on Terrorist Attacks upon the United States, *The 9/11 Commission Report: Final Report of the National Commission on Terrorist Attacks upon the United States*, New York: W. W. Norton & Company, 2004, available from *govinfo.library. unt.edu/911/report/911Report.pdf.*

21. For instance, see M. Ottaway and D. Kaysi, "The State of Iraq," Washington, DC: Carnegie Endowment for International Peace, February 2012, available from *carnegieendowment.org/files/ state_of_iraq.pdf*; C. Pascual and K. M. Pollack, "The Critical Battles: Reconciliation and Reconstruction in Iraq," *The Washington Quarterly*, Vol. 30, No. 3, 2007, pp. 7-19.

22. G. Bruno, "Iraq's Political Landscape," Washington, DC: Council on Foreign Policy Relations, 2009, available from *www. cfr.org/world/iraqs-political-landscape/p18411*; T. Dodge, "State and Society in Iraq Ten Years after Regime Change: The Rise of a

New Authoritarianism," *International Affairs*, Vol. 89, No. 2, 2013, pp. 241–257.

23. S. Kane, "Iraq's Oil Politics. Where Agreement Might be Found," Washington, DC: United States Institute for Peace, 2010, available from *www.usip.org/sites/default/files/resources/iraq_oil_ pw64.pdf*; "Iraq Report: Political Fragmentation and Corruption Stymie Economic Growth and Political Progress. A Minority Staff Trip Report to the Committee on Foreign Relations, United States Senate," Washington, DC: U.S. Committee on Foreign Relations, 2012, available from *www.gpo.gov/fdsys/*.

24. H. A. Hamoudi, "Identitarian Violence and Identitarian Politics: Elections and Governance in Iraq," *Harvard International Law Journal*, Vol. 51, 2010, pp. 82-95; F. Hadad, "The Politics of Sectarianism in Iraq," C. Spencer, J. Kinninmont, and O. Sirri, eds., *Iraq Ten Years On*, London, UK: Chatham House, 2013.

25. "Prospects for Further Proliferation of Nuclear Weapons," *Special National Intelligence Estimate*, August 23, 1974, p. 38, available from *www.fas.org/nuke/guide/snie4-1-74.pdf*. The precise nature of concern at this time seems to be hypothetical, as the report emphasizes that Iran's nuclear program is still entirely in its planning phase and merely states the assessment that there is no doubt, however, of the Shah's ambition to make Iran a power not to be reckoned with. If he is alive in the mid-1980s, if Iran has a full-fledged nuclear industry and all the facilities necessary for nuclear weapons, and if other countries have proceeded with nuclear weapons development, we have no doubt that Iran will follow suit.

A similar tenor is expressed in various other memos and notes, e.g., "Memorandum for the Assistant to the President for National Security Affairs: Department of State Response to NSSM 219 (Nuclear Cooperation with Iran)," April 18, 1975; see also Paul Kerr, "Iran's Nuclear Program: Status," *Congressional Research Service Report for Congress*, Washington, DC: Congressional Research Service, 2012, available from *www.fas.org/sgp/crs/nuke/ RL34544.pdf*.

26. *The Weapons Proliferation Threat*, Monterey, CA: Monterey Institute of International Studies, Nonproliferation Center, March 1995, p. 12, available from *www.dtic.mil/cgi-bin/ GetTRDoc?AD=ADA338686*.

27. Sharon Squassoni, "Iran's Nuclear Program: Recent Developments," *Congressional Research Service Report for Congress*, Washington, DC: Congressional Research Service, 2006, available from *www.dtic.mil/cgi-bin/GetTRDoc?Location=U2&doc=GetTRDoc.pdf&AD=ADA477711*. Newly elected Iranian President Hassan Rouhani again reaffirmed this in August 2013. J. Warrick, "Iran's Nuclear Program Is Making Steady Gains but Is Staying Below 'Red Line,' Report Says," *The Washington Post*, August 28, 2013.

28. Kerr, "Iran's Nuclear Program," p. 6.

29. The IAEA's latest available report also confirms the continuation of Iranian enrichment activities at the time of writing. IAEA Board of Governors, *Implementation of the NPT Safeguards Agreement and relevant provisions of Security Council resolutions in the Islamic Republic of Iran*, May 22, 2013, p. 3, available from *www.iaea.org/Publications/Documents/Board/2013/gov2013-6.pdf*.

30. U.S. sanctions against Iran are listed under U.S. Department of the Treasury, available from *www.treasury.gov/resource-center/sanctions/Programs/pages/iran.aspx*. For an overview, see M. Kinaci, "Tightening Oil Sanctions on Iran," *Journal of Energy Studies*, August 7, 2012.

31. Kerr, "Iran's Nuclear Program," pp. 24-26; IAEA Board of Governors; "Sanctions Cost Iran $40Bn in 2012, IEA Says," *Middle East Economic Survey*, Vol. 56, No. 7, February 15, 2013.

32. Author's personal interview with local security staff and local intelligentsia, Abu Dhabi and Dubai, April-May 2013, and London, UK, July 2013. See also C. Ferris-Ley, "Saudi Prince Warns of Middle East Nuclear Arms Race," *Arabian Business*, January 26, 2012. For a recent perspective, see S. Maloney, "Thinking the Unthinkable: The Gulf States and the Prospect of Nuclear Iran," Middle East Memo, Washington, DC: The Brookings Institute, 2013, available from *www.brookings.edu/~/media/Research/Files/Papers/2013/1/25%20iran%20maloney/0125_iran_maloney.pdf*.

33. "Straits of Hormuz" in *World Oil Transit Chokepoints*, Washington, DC: EIA, 2011, available from *www.eia.gov/countries/regions-topics.cfm?fips=WOTC#hormuz*.

34. "Global Oil Choke Points," Montgomery, AL: Lehman Brothers Global Equity Research, January 18, 2008; "Dire Straits," *LNG Intelligence,* January 11, 2011; Jean-Paul Rodrigue, "Straits, Passages, and Chokepoints: A Maritime Geostrategy of Petroleum Distribution," *Les Cahiers de Géographie du Quebec* (*Geography Papers of Quebec*), Vol. 48, No. 135, 2004; Caitlin Talmadge, "Closing Time. Assessing the Iranian Threat to the Strait of Hormuz," *International Security,* Vol. 33, No. 1, Summer 2008, pp. 82–117; D. Blair and K. Lieberthal, "Smooth Sailing: The World's Shipping Lanes Are Safe," *Foreign Affairs,* May-June, 2007.

35. Individual country statistics show the rising value of oil revenues, which account for between 70 and 98 percent of GCC countries' total governmental revenues. For example, see for Saudi Arabia's case: *Annual Statistics 2012,* Jeddah, Saudi Arabia: Saudi Arabian Monetary Agency, 2013, available from *www.sama. gov.sa/sites/samaen/ReportsStatistics/statistics/Pages/YearlyStatistics.aspx.* For regional perspectives, see *Global Economic Prospects. Navigating Strong Currents,* Vol. II, Washington, DC: World Bank, 2011, pp. 95-105.

36. The 5-year compound average growth rate between 2007 and 2011 for the GCC economies was 4.6 percent, about half of developing Asia's 8.8 percent over the same period, but more than five times the growth in the EU (0.6 percent) and other advanced economies (0.7 percent). QNB, *GCC Economic Insight 2012,* available from *www.qnb.com.qa/cs/Satellite?blobcol=urldata&blobheader= application2Fpdf&blobkey=id&blobtable=MungoBlobs&blobwhere=1 35549637828&ssbinary=true,* p. 13. See also IMF, *World Economic Outlook 2010. Rebalancing Growth,* Washington DC: International Monetary Fund, 2010, pp. 61-67; IMF, *World Economic Outlook 2013. Hopes, Realities, Risks,* Washington DC: International Monetary Fund, 2010, pp. 59-64.

37. B. Haykel, "Saudi Arabia and Qatar in a Time of Revolution," Gulf Analysis Paper, Washington, DC: Center for Strategic and International Studies, February 2013; L. Khatib, "Qatar's Foreign Policy: The Limits of Pragmatism," *International Affairs,* Vol. 89, No. 2, 2013, pp. 417–431.

38. Khatib; Christopher Blanchard, *Qatar: Background and U.S. Relations,* Report RL31718, Washington, DC: Congressional Research Service, May 16, 2011; Haykel.

39. Haykel. In august 2013, the Saudi King called for the international community to abstain from interfering in Egypt's domestic affairs after the military deposed Muslim Brotherhood-backed President Morsi. Al-Sharq Al-Awsat, "Al-Saudiyah tada`u al-mujtama` al-dawli li-tafham mudhamin risalat khadim al-haramain haula misr" ("Saudi Arabia calls on International Community to Understand the content of the Custodian of the two Holy Mosques' letter regarding Egypt"), August 20, 2013.

40. K. Katzman, "The United Arab Emirates (UAE): Issues for U.S. Policy," *Congressional Research Service Report for Congress,* Washington, DC: Congressional Research Service, 2013.

41. *Ibid.*

42. The UAE's nuclear reactors stand under strict IAEA safeguards; among other commitments, the UAE will not enrich uranium itself, relying instead on imported, enriched fuel. "Abu Dhabi Moves Ahead With Nuclear Program," *Middle East Economic Survey,* Vol. 55, No. 34, August 20, 2012; D. Knott, "UAE Secures $2Bn Ex-Im Bank Loan To Buy U.S. Nuclear Equipment," *Middle East Economic Survey,* Vol. 55, No. 38, September 14, 2012.

43. "KPMG Emerging Trends in the Sovereign Wealth Fund Landscape. Middle East," p. 4, available from *www.kpmg.com/AE/ en/Documents/2013/Emerging_trends_in_the_regional_SWF_landscape.pdf.* These numbers appear in line with other previous estimates, for instance, Brad Setser and Rachel Ziemba, "GCC Sovereign Funds Reversal of Fortune," Working Paper, Washington, DC: Council on Foreign Relations, 2009, p. 2.

44. P. Kohler, "GCC Sovereign Wealth Funds: Leveraging Local Economic Development?" *World Economic Situation and Prospects Weekly Highlights,* 2013, available from *www.un.org/en/development/desa/policy/wesp/wesp_wh/wesp_wh16.pdf.*

45. Nader Habibi and Eckart Woertz, "US-Arab Economic Relations and the Obama Administration," Middle East Brief, No. 34, Waltham, MA: Brandeis University, February 2009.

46. G. Hussain, "Will the Middle East End Up Missing 'U.S. Imperialism'?" *The Commentator*, June 6, 2013.

47. For instance, see "IMF Regional Economic Outlook: Asia and Pacific. Shifting Risks, New Foundations for Growth," Washington DC: International Monetary Fund, 2013, available from *www.imf.org/external/pubs/ft/reo/2013/APD/eng/areo0413.pdf*. See also "IMF World Economic Outlook 2013," Washington DC: International Monetary Fund, 2013, pp. 19-24, available from *www.imf.org/external/pubs/ft/weo/2013/01/pdf/text.pdf*.

48. "IEA Global Energy Outlook 2012," Paris, France: International Energy Agency, 2012.

49. "EIA Country Analysis Briefs for Saudi Arabia, Kuwait, the UAE, Oman, and Qatar," available from *www.eia.gov/countries/*.

50. Bassam Fattouh and Jonathan Stern, *Natural Gas Markets in the Middle East and North Africa*, Oxford, UK: Oxford University Press, 2011, available from *www.oxfordenergy.org/shop/natural-gas-markets-in-the-middle-east-and-north-africa/*.

51. A. A. Aluweisheg, "The GCC Turns East," *Arab News*, December 9, 2012.

52. *Ibid.*

53. *EIA Country Analysis Briefs for China, Japan and South Korea*, available from *www.eia.gov/countries/*.

54. E.g., see Christopher Davidson, "Persian Gulf—Pacific Asia Linkages in the 21st Century: A Marriage of Convenience?" London, UK: London School of Economics and Political Science, Kuwait Program on Development, Governance and Globalisation in the Gulf States, 2010; Thierry Kellner, "The GCC States of the Persian Gulf and Asia Energy Relations," IFRI Note, Brussels, Belgium: French Institute of International Relations (IFRI), 2012.

55. C. Stanton, "Abu Dhabi Signs Nuclear Power Deal with South Korean Group," *The National*, December 28, 2009.

56. M. Al-Asoomi, "China Breaks West's Solar Monopoly," *Gulf News*, May 24, 2012.

57. Davidson, p. 2.

58. Michael Peel and Camilla Hall, "Abu Dhabi Pushes for Homegrown Defence," *Financial Times*, February 25, 2013, available from *www.ft.com/cms/s/0/1ac60098-7f2d-11e2-89ed-00144feabd c0.html#axzz2dTNxSJGc*; James Doran, "Home-Grown Defence Companies at Abu Dhabi's Tawazun Industrial Park," *The National*, February 19, 2013, available from *www.thenational.ae/ business/economy/home-grown-defence-companies-at-abu-dhabis-tawa-zun-industrial-park*.

59. *Popular Protest in North Africa and the Middle East (VIII): Bahrain's Rocky Road to Reform*, Middle East Report No. 111, Vol. 12, Brussels, Belgium: International Crisis Group (ICG), pp. 3-9, available from *www.crisisgroup.org/en/regions/middle-east-north-africa/iraq-iran-gulf/bahrain/111-popular-protest-in-north-africa-and-the-middle-east-viii-bahrains-rocky-road-to-reform.aspx*. The event was also investigated under a separate commission: Bahrain Independent Commission of Inquiry (2011), *Report of the Bahrain Independent Commission of Inquiry*, Presented in Manama, Bahrain, November 23, 2011, available from *www.bici.org.bh/ BICIreportEN.pdf*.

60. ICG, pp. 3, 21.

61. The U.S. Government did react in some ways, condemning individual acts and sending delegates and commissioners to Bahrain in addition to direct phone calls, including by Obama, urging Bahrain toward "meaningful reform that is responsive to the aspirations of all Bahrainis." See U.S. State Department's daily press releases for April 30, 2013 ("President Obama's call with the King of Bahrain"), March 30, 2011 and April 18, 2013, available from *www.state.gov*.

62. U.S. Joint Chiefs of Staff, *The National Military Strategy of the United States*, Washington, DC: U.S. Department of Defense.

63. Edward Cody, "First French Military Base Opens in the Persian Gulf," *The Washington Post*, May 27, 2009, available from *articles.washingtonpost.com/2009-05-27/world/36882134_1_rafale-french-soldiers-first-military-base*.

64. "Livre Blanc Defence et Securite Nationale" ("White Paper on Defence and National Security"), Direction de l'information légale et administrative (Directorate of Legal and Administrative Information), Paris, France, 2013, available from *www.ladocumentationfrancaise.fr/var/storage/rapports-publics/134000257/0000.pdf*.

65. Frank Gardner, "East of Suez: Are UK forces Returning?" *BBC News*, April 23, 2013, available from *www.bbc.co.uk/news/uk-22333555*.

66. Haykel, 2013.

67. Fawaz A. Gerges, "The Obama Approach to the Middle East: The End of America's Moment?" *International Affairs*, Vol. 89, No. 2, 2013, pp. 299–323, especially p. 301. The presidential quote is taken from Part 3 of a CNN Democratic presidential debate, CNN, January 21, 2008.

68. For more on this topic, see Mohammed El-Katiri, *The Future of the Arab Gulf Monarchies in the Age of Uncertainties*, Carlisle, PA: Strategic Studies Institute, U.S. Army War College, June 2013.

69. Office of the Press Secretary, "President Barack Obama's inaugural address," Washington, DC: The White House, January 21, 2009, available from *www.whitehouse.gov/blog/inaugural-address/*.

70. Indyk, p. 27; see also K. M. Pollack, "Security in the Persian Gulf: New Frameworks for the Twenty-First Century," Middle East Memo, Washington, DC: The Brookings Institute, 2012, available from *www.brookings.edu/research/papers/2012/06/middle-east-pollack*.

U.S. ARMY WAR COLLEGE

Major General William E. Rapp
Commandant

*****

STRATEGIC STUDIES INSTITUTE
and
U.S. ARMY WAR COLLEGE PRESS

Director
Professor Douglas C. Lovelace, Jr.

Director of Research
Dr. Steven K. Metz

Author
Dr. Mohammed El-Katiri

Editor for Production
Dr. James G. Pierce

Publications Assistant
Ms. Rita A. Rummel

*****

Composition
Mrs. Jennifer E. Nevil